I0560300

The Chamoru American Warrior

Aaron Quitugua

Hinanao Press

Chamoru History

Chamoru History:

The Chamoru people are the Indigenous Pacific Islanders of all Mariana Islands in the Western Pacific Micronesia region. Guam/Guahan, Rota/Luta, Saipan, and Tinian are the most populated islands of the archipelago. According to Chamoru culture, our creation story began from Fouha rock. The story of Gods (Puntan and Fu'una) who were siblings. Modern theories say we belong to a distinct group of Pacific Islanders in Oceania, with an age of nearly 5,000 years (newer theories suggest nearly 7,000+ years). To compare human history timelines, we are one of the oldest Pacific Islanders of remote Oceania, if not the eldest. Our people are older than nearly all Egyptian pyramids.

Apart from loanwords gained through contact with external cultures and populations who introduced novel resources (e.g., chickens, pigs, water buffalo) and practices, the Chamoru people and language developed largely in isolation. Creating its own independent branch within the Western Malayo-Polynesian family of the Austronesion Oceanic language tree. Our language has no mutually intelligible extant-related language.

Chamorus are known for multiple achievements. Besides being one of the oldest sea voyaging peoples of remote Oceania, we had one of the fastest hand-built sea vessels (Galaide) available, and created our own megaliths known as latte Stones. Some latte stones are older than Mayan pyramids. The latte stone, carved from limestone or basalt, comprises a base pillar and a cylindrical capstone. They can range in size from "3 ft" to nearly "30 ft" tall, and can weigh from "a couple hundred pounds to 60+ tons,". They are used in a set (4 to 14) for home foundations that lift our homes (Guma Latte) and people out of the harsh island environments. Some houses were "12 ft" wide and "48 ft" long with some latte stones still standing today. One. standing at the Bishop Museum in Hawaii. The latte stones serve as symbols of strength and resilience to us, Chamorus.

We have endured multiple extinction-level events throughout our long history. Having fought two world superpowers (Spain and Japan), we are still here. Although, it did not come without a cost. Historians estimated native Chamorus lost nearly 95% of our total population by the end of our resistance period. The total native population dwindled from almost 100,000 to nearly 5,000. We suffered multiple forms of colonization, such as direct rule, forced religious conversions, and imposing social and cultural changes. Some of the remaining population realized converting to Catholicism was better than eventual death and took Spanish names as part of religious confirmation.

Since the early 16th century (nearly 400 years ago), the Spaniards occupied the Mariana Islands. Through Spaniard accounts, the average Chamoru man was of muscular build and nearly "5 ft 10 in" tall (historical accounts of "10 ft" tall Chamorus - Chief Taga). Compared to the Spaniards, whose average male height was "5 ft" to "5 ft 2 in". During the Spanish-Chamoru War, Chamorus fought with slings and spears (sometimes made of human bone). Whereas the Spaniards had their outside diseases and rifles. When the Spaniards encountered traditional Chamoru practices that did not follow Catholic doctrine or approve of, they would categorize them as heresy, idolatry, and ban the practice.

Slowly, stripping away our native customs and traditions for Catholicisms accepted practices.

The Spaniards lost to the United States during the Spanish-American War in 1898. Guam and the rest of the Mariana Islands split up. Guam went to the Americans and Spain sold the Northern Mariana Islands to Germany. Chamorus initially welcomed the Americans with hope for progress and protection. Still, a long period of military rule offered little in the way of rights or meaningful development. From 1898 to 1950, the U.S. treated Guam less than a community and more like a strategic military outpost in the Pacific. The U.S. Navy controlled the island, and its governors were naval officers with absolute authority. Chamorus were only seen as U.S. "nationals" but not citizens. This meant Chamorus had no right to vote, no representation in Congress, and no constitutional protections. Under this naval government, Americanization became policy.

Americans suppressed Chamoru culture, language, and traditions in favor of English-language education, introduced Protestantism, and loyalty to the United States. The U.S. Navy rewrote local laws, established new education and health systems, and emphasized military discipline and order. Chamorus wound up being treated as second-class residents on our islands. Although there were improvements in sanitation, health, and education, the American changes filtered through a paternalistic lens that denied local participation in governance. The people of Guam had no say in their leaders and all authority rested with the naval governors.

The other extinction level event would be the

nearly three-year-long Japanese occupation of our islands during World War II. On December 8, 1941 (Chamoru Standard Time), after the attack on Pearl Harbor, Japanese forces invaded Guam. The majority of the occupation lasted between December 10, 1941–July 21, 1944. Guam was incorporated into Japan's South Seas Mandate and was administered by the Japanese military. On July 21, 1944, the U.S. launched a major amphibious assault to retake the island during the Battle of Guam, part of the Mariana and Palau Islands campaign. After heavy fighting, U.S. forces, with the help of the newly formed active duty and an all-native freedom fighter group known as the Guam Combat Patrol, regained complete liberation of the island. The battle resulted in significant casualties on both sides, including many Chamoru civilians. During the Occupation of Guam, a majority of nearly 22,000 Chamorus suffered atrocities at the hands of the Japanese. Although records show that nearly 1,200 Chamoru lives were lost, the actual number may be way higher.

During World War II, the U.S. forces defending Guam were minimal and surrendered early. This left Chamorus defenseless when Japan invaded in December 1941. The brutal 3 year Japanese Occupation killed many Chamorus through massacres, forced labor, starvation, and abuse. Despite the feeling of abandonment, Chamorus remained loyal to the United States. The retaking of Guam in 1944 by the U.S. involved heavy bombardment, leaving the island devastated. In the aftermath, without local input, reconstruction efforts prioritized military infrastructure over civilian needs. Chamorus still lacked citizenship and political rights, and frustrations mounted.

From the period between the end of the war and the passaging of the Organic Act of 1950, growing demands for civil rights and recognition began to spark. Chamorus, having endured colonization by three empires and wartime suffering, began organizing for self-governance and U.S. citizenship. Loyalty and sacrifice during World War II became a pillar for the argument. Ultimately, in 1950, the U.S. Congress passed the Guam Organic Act, which granted U.S. citizenship to the people of Guam. This retroactively gave citizenship to all Chamorus born from 1899 to the present (1950) and established a civilian government. However, this did not provide full political equality, as Guam remained an unincorporated territory with limited self-rule and no voting representation in Congress. Guam has the highest military service enlistment rate per capita in the United States. One-third of our prime land is occupied by U.S. Military bases.

Preface

Preface:

Francisco Jesus Cruz (Family: Felisa Cruz from Asan), also known as Kiko or Ton Kiko, was 21 years old when the Japanese Occupation began. Cruz was born on June 5, 1920, in Guam and was one of nine children to his father, Joaquin Cruz Cruz, and his mother, Rosa Limtiaco Jesus Cruz. He married Julita Cruz Leon Guerrero, and they had nine kids after the war. My amazing grandmother, Ruthann Cruz, is their daughter. My father is Cruz's oldest grand, and my brothers and I are his oldest great-grands.

I wrote this book in honor of the the Guam Combat Patrol and my great-grandfather, a native born Chamoru freedom fighter whose courage during the Liberation of Guam earned him the promise of the Medal of Honor from Admiral Chester Nimitz. Though our government's promise was never fulfilled, his heroic actions fighting behind enemy lines saved countless military and civilian lives. The story of the Battle of Guam and the fight for our island's freedom should remain etched in the memory of all who call America home.

As one of his descendants, I carry the torch of his legacy. This book is both a tribute and a call to action. A way to share his story with the world and continue the effort to see our country, the United States, finally award him the Medal of Honor he so rightfully deserves. Although now posthumously, he would still be the first Chamoru, the first Pacific Islander American, to be promised or receive such recognition if granted. It is not only an honor, it is our history. His blood ran for the freedom of Guam. He helped achieve the broader American mission, operation Forager. His courage deserves more than silence.

Preface:

Cruz with his wife Julita. (Photo credit: Personal Collection)

Introduction

Introduction:

The Battle of Guam in 1944 was a turning point in the Pacific Theater of World War II. It was a strategic victory for American Forces reclaiming a U.S. territory after nearly three years of brutal Japanese Occupation. Behind the widely told stories of amphibious landings, aerial bombardments, and U.S. Marines raising the flag lies a quieter, often erased chapter. The story of the native Chamoru people who suffered, resisted, and fought alongside the U.S. Marines for our homeland's liberation.

Guam, the largest and the southernmost island of the Mariana Islands archipelago, became both battleground and prison when Japanese forces invaded just hours after Pearl Harbor. For 31 months, the Chamoru population endured forced labor, starvation, torture, and mass executions. Many civilians risked their lives hiding American sailors (Medal of Freedom recipient George Tweed), resisting in secret, and sabotaging enemy movements. Some paid with their lives. Others, like my great-grandfather, became legends in whispers. Passed down by survivors. Remembered not in history books but in the hearts of families and villages.

Introduction:

The broader narrative of World War II often overlooks the heroic acts of native resistance and sacrifices. Histories of the Pacific War spotlight generals, admirals, and geopolitical movements. Even well-meaning mainstream accounts of Guam's Liberation rarely go beyond the perspective of the U.S. military, leaving the Chamoru people as silent backdrops rather than central figures in our liberation. Our courage, losses, and loyalty deserve to be seen, heard, and honored. This book aims to change that.

This book isn't just a tribute to the Guam Combat Patrol or my Medal of Honor promised great-grandfather. It is a call to acknowledge the Chamoru role in World War II with dignity and truth. His story is unique in its courage, but it is rare in how close it came to the fruition of the promise. And yet, like too many unsung heroes, his name inching closer to being lost to the tide of war and time.

Now, as generations move further from the war and fewer witnesses remain, there is an urgency in telling these stories. These stories are not just history, they are legacy. It is identity. It is justice long delayed. By revisiting the Battle of Guam through the eyes of its native defenders, we remember that freedom was not just reclaimed by troops who landed on the beaches. Acknowledging the tenacity of the Chamoru people, who refused to yield and helped safeguard our continuity.

Chapter 1- Marianas Before War

Chapter 1: Marianas Before War

Besides the nearly 4,500 years before colonization reached the Mariana Islands shores, the islands thrived with a rich Pacific Islander culture. For millennium, Chamoru life has been dictated by the rhythm of the tides and seasons. Villages stretched across the coastline and inland jungles. Families (Mangåfa) lived together, sharing labor, food, and customs passed down through generations. Fishing, farming, and community gatherings formed the rhythm of daily life. Respect for elders (manåmko'), devotion to family, and deep connection to the moon (Pulan), land (Tåno), and ocean (Tåsi) defined the Chamoru identity.

Homes were simple, functional, and extremely sturdy. Made from deeply pitched roofs, thatch buildings, wooden beams, and carved-out latte stone foundations. Men fished off-shore with handmade nets or spears, built canoes from breadfruit (Lemmai), and trained for warfare and navigation. In contrast, women fished near the shore, cultivated crops (coconut, rice, taro, bananas), weaved, made pottery, and cared for the household. Elders taught younger generations about ancestral values. Nature was not just a resource, it was sacred and inhabited by the spirits of our ancient ancestors (Taotaomo'na), who can guide or harm the living. This was life for the Chamoru people before colonial hands redrew the map.

However, the ambitions of world superpowers long disrupted the peaceful life of the Mariana Islands. First, came Spain (Magellan) in 1521. Spain claimed Guam in 1565 (Legazpi) and colonized the Marianas completely after the last battle of the Chamoru-Spanish War in 1699. Spain began converting the population to Catholicism in 1668, disrupting indigenous governance, banning parts of ancient Chamoru practices/customs, and renaming places with Spanish designations. Chamorus lived under Spanish rule for nearly 4 centuries, and our way of life altered but never erased.

The Treaty of Paris ceded Guam to the United States in 1898, following the Spanish-American War. Overnight, Chamorus went from subjects of the former premier world superpower to subjects under a rising American empire. The U.S. Navy assumed control of the island, establishing it as a coaling station and strategic military outpost. Yet, for the Chamoru people, this transition did not come with the rights or protections of U.S. citizenship. We were looked down upon and disparaged. Naval rule governed us. Which excluded Chamorus from voting and representation, while military governors, with ultimate authority over all island matters, issued orders to all.

Throughout these events, many Chamorus remained hopeful. Embracing education, learned English (spoke Chamoru at home or privately), and adapted to the changes brought by the American presence. Americanism, Spanish, and Chamoru customs forcefully blended. As this progressed, the natives began to speak out for themselves and advocate for more autonomy and civil rights. Guam and eventually the rest of the Mariana Islands became a complex mosaic of Chamoru in ethnicity, Spanish in faith, and American in law.

Unbeknownst to the natives, Guam's geographical location made it a pawn in a global conflict. As tensions rose in the Pacific, Guam's strategic value as a U.S. territory made it a target for the empire of Japan. Chamorus, without citizenship, military protection, and little understanding of the storm approaching, was about to be caught in the crossfire of powers far beyond their shores. The upcoming storm will again test the resilience of every Chamoru value, tradition, and soul in the Marianas.

Chapter 1: Marianas Before War

View along street of pre-war Assan. (Photo Credit: National Park Services)

Chapter 2- Japanese Occupation

Chapter 2: Japanese Occupation

Cruz lived a fairly quiet and honest life in the days before the darkness of war swallowed Guam. A sturdy man with calloused hands and a steady heart. He worked as a dynamiter at the Assan Point rock quarry. Where the earth cracked open with every controlled blast and revealed the bones of the island. Life was hard but familiar. It was defined by hard labor, family, and beautiful scenery of the island.

But war has a way of interrupting peace like a sudden typhoon. It came to the Mariana Islands not as a whisper but as a roar. News spread quickly in the last hours before the Japanese arrived on Guam. The chatter of fear swept through villages like wind through the coconut trees. Cruz's work supervisor pulled him aside and said, "Hide the dynamite, they'll take it if you don't". And so Cruz did.

With the enemy on the horizon, he acted swiftly. He moved through the jungles of Assan with a quickness. He knew the jungle like the lines on his own hands. Nearly 700 sticks of dynamite, enough to level a hill, vanished into the earth. Hidden in a secret cache only he knew. It was a risk to his life and everyone around him. If caught, they would torture, execute, and make an example of him. Although a daunting task, Cruz was no ordinary man. And the Japanese were about to meet no ordinary enemy.

Chapter 2: Japanese Occupation

On December 8, 1941, just hours after the attack on Pearl Harbor, war engulfed Guam. Without a substantial U.S. military presence to defend the island, Japanese bombers quickly took to the skies over Hagåtña. They targeted the Marine barracks, the naval yard at Sumai, and the island's few airstrips. The Chamoru people, waking to the thunder of warplanes and the distant sounds of exploding shells, could hardly understand the scale of the global conflict now crashing onto their shores.

Within two days, Japanese troops landed on Guam, through the five bays of Ylig, Malesso, Humåtak, Tumon, and Hagåtña. The Japanese troops overwhelmed Guam's small U.S. garrison of barely 500 men. On December 10, Captain George J. McMillin, Guam's 38th and final Naval Governor, officially surrendered. The Stars and Stripes came down, and in its place rose the red sun of the Japanese Empire. The Japanese Empire renamed Guam *"Omiya-Jima"*, which meant Great Shrine Island. For the next 31 months, the Chamoru people endured one of the harshest occupations in the Pacific.

Chapter 2: Japanese Occupation

Imperial Japanese soldiers outside the former U.S. Marine Barracks in Sumai during the Japanese occupation of Guam. (Photo Credit: National Park Services)

Chapter 2: Japanese Occupation

Japanese sentries standing guard in force occupied Chamoru family homes.
(Photo Credit: National Park Services)

Chapter 2: Japanese Occupation

Upon arrival, the South Seas Detachment of the Imperial Japanese Army imposed martial law and banned public gatherings. They forced Chamorus to bow to Japanese officers, learn the Japanese language, and abandon American customs. The Japanese army seized schools and converted them into indoctrination centers. Communication methods were confiscated and dissent met with swift and brutal punishment.

Japanese troops repurposed entire villages into labor camps. Soldiers forced men to build airstrips, dig trenches, and carry ammunition. Women were forced to work as cooks and tend the farms. Some suffered worse fates, as they were raped and beaten. They had to mask their suffered psychological scars and fear in order to survive. Everyone under the constant threat of being beaten and executed. The war did not spare the elderly, sick, or young. Japanese soldiers received rice, sugar, and other supplies through rationing or redirection, leaving many families malnourished. Soldiers seized the livestock and banned fishing in certain areas. Hunger and death became a daily torment.

The Japanese used fear tactics as their weapon. Beheadings, public executions, and disappearances became common. For a single act of resistance, the Japanese punished entire families. The Manenggon Concentration Camp, hastily built in July 1944, became a symbol of the empires desperation and cruelty. In the last weeks before Guam's Liberation, the Japanese marched over 18,000 Chamorus there. Many were already weakened by hunger or illness. Some never returned. The Chamoru spirit, however, did not break.

Chapter 2: Japanese Occupation

Chamoru women, younger children, and elderly were forced to work in the rice paddies, growing food for the Japanese Army. (Photo Credit: National Park Services)

Chapter 3- Battle of Guam

Chapter 3: Battle of Guam

In the early months of 1944, the U.S. intensified its efforts to reclaim our territories lost to Japan, with Guam emerging as a strategic priority. The Mariana Islands strategic location made it an ideal base for launching operations deeper into Japanese-held territories. Operation Forager was the plan created to establish airfields for the new B-29 Superfortress bombers. Included in this plan, was the recapture of the Mariana and Palau Islands.

Admiral Chester W. Nimitz, was the Commander of the Pacific Fleet and orchestrated the campaign. He designating Admiral Raymond A. Spruance to lead the Fifth Fleet and oversee the Central Pacific Task Force. The initial schedule set the invasion of Guam for June 18, 1944. Shortly after the assault on Saipan. However, fierce resistance on Saipan and the consequential Battle of the Philippine Sea (Great Marianas Turkey Shoot) caused a postponement. This allowed U.S. forces to regroup and intensify their preparatory bombardments on Guam.

Chapter 3: Battle of Guam

From mid-June to July 1944, the Americans subjected Guam to extensive aerial and naval bombardments. Carrier-based aircraft and B-24 bombers targeted Japanese defenses. Battleships and cruisers shelled the island's fortifications. A lot of these bombings destroyed local Chamoru communities almost completely. However, these attacks aimed to weaken Japanese positions and disrupt supply lines. By doing so, it helped set the stage for the amphibious assault.

The American recapture forces is composed of 55,000 troops. Those forces included the 3rd Marine Division, 1st Provisional Marine Brigade, and the U.S. Army's 77th Infantry Division. On July 21, 1944, these forces landed on Guam's western beaches of Assan and Hågat. They faced entrenched Japanese defenders who had fortified the island with bunkers, artillery emplacements, and natural obstacles.

The recapture of Guam was not only a significant military victory, it was symbolic. For the Chamoru people, it marked the near end of a brutal occupation and the restoration of our homeland. For the U.S., it regained a lost pre-war territory and provided a critical base for launching further operations in the Pacific. By bringing the war closer to Japan's doorstep, Operation Forager helped lead to the events of the two atomic bombs being dropped from one of our Chamoru islands, Tinian.

Chapter 3: Battle of Guam

By July 1944, American forces were landing on Guam to liberate the island. Japanese troops knew their defeat was near and feared Chamoru collaboration with the Americans. Many Chamorus maintained loyalty to the U.S. and quietly supported American return. This loyalty angered and alarmed the Japanese, who viewed the locals as a threat.

As U.S. troops approached, the Japanese began moving villagers inland to the Asinan and Manenggon concentration camps to control and monitor them. During these forced marches, Japanese soldiers separated villagers. They often took the largest/tallest men, most educated, or the most outspoken, under false pretenses.

Japanese commanders, under immense pressure, ordered executions to prevent any uprising or support for the Americans. The killings sent a message to break the Chamoru spirit. There were multiple mass executions and specific incidents like Tinta and Faha. At Tinta, Japanese soldiers told 30 villagers they were being moved for safety. They were then confined in a cave and attacked with grenades and machetes. Sixteen were killed; others survived by pretending to be dead. At Faha, 46 villagers were gathered and massacred; none survived.

Chapter 3: Battle of Guam

U.S. Marines of the Third Marine Division continued to come ashore. (Photo Courtesy: NPS National Archive 80-G-238991)

Chapter 3: Battle of Guam

First American flag on Guam after recapture operations initiated. (Assan Beach) (National Archives Identifier 532532)

Chapter 4- Medal of Honor Heroics

Chapter 4: Medal of Honor Heroics

Japanese forces swept across Guam. They imposing their rule by rifle point, bayonets, and banners. After finding out the Japanese had already captured his parents, Cruz disappeared into the wild jungles of Assan. Deep the jungle, he built a hidden hideout. The hideout was a blend of concealment, resourcefulness, and instinct. The site, hidden by leaves, trees, and branches, proved to be safe. In this concealed position, Cruz's status changed from quarry dynamiter to shadow warrior.

Night after night, under the cover of darkness, he emerged from the jungle like a ghost. He moved in silence, stalking lone Japanese soldiers who strayed too far from their posts. One by one, he took them. Each kill buried either beneath the jungle's blanket or discreetly interred in his parents land in Chalan Pago, where he made a secret cemetery. No witnesses. No mercy. It was just quiet vengeance from a man defending his homeland.

Every act of resistance was a gamble. Every moment spent alive was a moment borrowed. Yet, Cruz continued. Alone and armed with a knife, he would save what he could scavenge. He became a legend and a phantom feared by the occupiers. They could never find the source of their losses.

Chapter 4: Medal of Honor Heroics

One day, a strange twist of fate brought Cruz face to face with a sympathetic and vital voice. Alberto Tenorio, the father of Froilan Tenorio (4th Governor of the Northern Marianas) from Saipan. The Japanese forced him to serve as an interpreter. He then secretly sought out to Cruz. Though bound by the end of a rifle, Tenorio's heart remained loyal to his people.

Tears in his eyes, Tenorio said, "The Americans were coming, and the Japanese soldiers manning the big guns on Nimitz Hill were going to annihilate the Guamanian people in the Manenggon and Asinan concentration camps after annihilating the landing forces."

Tenorio painted a genocidal picture. The Japanese had fortified Asan's hills (Nimitz Hill Area) with artillery, multiple machine gun bunkers, and turned the slopes into deathtraps. Underground caves housed their command centers. Hundreds of combatants armed themselves, dug in, and were prepared to die. Cruz knew he had to act.

Chapter 4: Medal of Honor Heroics

As the sun rose over the waters of July 21, 1944, the horizon filled with steel. The 3rd Marine Division stormed the beaches of Assan and were met by a wall of gunfire and explosions. The hillside erupted into violence. Men fell in waves. Machine guns raked the sands. The Japanese had turned Assan into a fortress and they were exacting a brutal toll.

From his outpost area, Cruz watched it all. His heart pounded as he saw the young Marines falter. Their suffering was slow and excruciating. The pile of bodies began to rise. This continued wave after wave until the Marines retreated to the beaches to regroup. Then something unexpected happened.

He noticed the Japanese celebrating. In a grave miscalculation, the Japanese believed they had repelled the invasion. Saki filled cups and laughter rang through the caves. The nearly 800 soldiers who were confident in their victory, abandoned their fighting positions to celebrate underground. Only a single sentry remained to guard the fighting positions. The ten empty machine gun bunkers stared uselessly at the sea. Cruz's eyes locked on. This was the chance he had realized. It was now or never.

Chapter 4: Medal of Honor Heroics

Cruz crept forward like a wraith through the jungle with a satchel of dynamite. Step by agonizing step, heartbeat in his ears, he approached the lone sentry. In one sudden, savage moment, he struck silent, swift, and final. The sentry crumpled. Cruz stripped the uniform from the man and donned it himself.

Cruz became hard to detect, now camouflaged in the enemy's uniform blouse. He worked quickly while planting charges in the enemy's command cave and machine-gun nests. The risk was total. The discovery meant death. But fate was with him. Hours passed. Then the Marines began a renewed push. Hearing the thundering advance, the Japanese broke their celebration and rushed back to their positions right into Cruz's trap.

From a distance, he waited until the hill once again brimmed with soldiers and machine gunners. Then Cruz detonated every charge with the weight of his homeland behind him. The hillside exploded in a storm of fire, stone, and steel. Shaking the earth, the command cave collapsed and entombed hundreds. The machine-gun nests vaporized and the tide of battle turned in an instant. Americans could finally push forward. What they did not know and what history nearly forgot, was that one man watching from the jungle with 700 sticks of dynamite and an iron will just saved 100's, 1,000's, or more American and Chamoru lives.

With the extreme amounts of lives taken during his heroic actions, Cruz kept his actions a secret from the public. At first, the only people who Cruz told or found out were the higher chain of command Marines, Admiral Chester Nimitz, and close family/friends. After Admiral Nimitz heard, he promised Cruz the Medal of Honor award. Colonel Miller, the commanding offer of the Marine barracks in Guam heard of the actions and grew great respect for Cruz which led to a long lasting friendship. Unfortunately, during the first day fighting in the islands recapture, Col. Miller was wounded causing his evacuation for treatment.

Faced with an empire, Cruz fought the only way he knew he could. In the jungle's silence, he carried the weight of a nation. In the explosions that shattered the Assan hillside, he left a legacy that echoes throughout all generations. Weaving his inspirational combat actions into the living history of the Chamoru people and our enduring spirit. He was not a soldier yet but his island needed a hero. Although he lacked military training, Cruz became fire, shadow, and salvation. And that, perhaps, is the greatest kind of hero.

Chapter 4: Medal of Honor Heroics

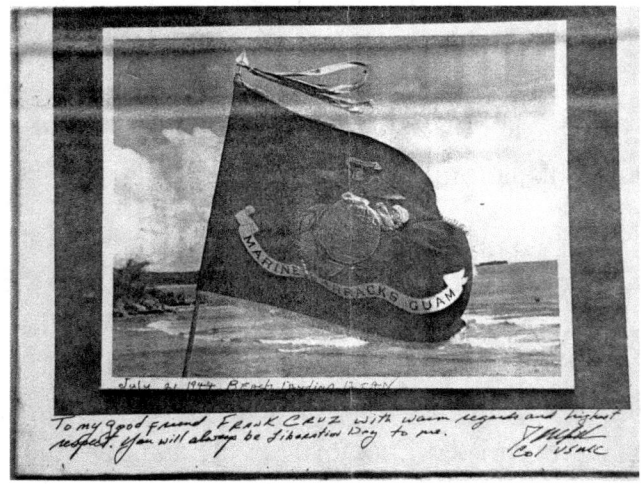

Cruz's letter from Col. Miller. (Photo credit: Personal Collection).

Chapter 5- Continued Liberation with GCP

Chapter 5: Continued Liberation with GCP

Although the official declaration of Guam's Liberation came in August 1944, fighting persisted. Hidden in the island's deep jungles, caves, and swamps were remnants of the once formidable Japanese garrison. Soldiers too loyal to surrender and too proud to dishonor their emperor. These stragglers waged a silent and deadly resistance long after the battle lines had disappeared.

Stolen U.S. fatigues were what the remaining Japanese forces would wear. They scavenged through military dumps and anywhere else for weapons, ammunition, and food. Signs of their presence included discarded bodies, stolen resources, mysterious foot prints, and disturbed brush. They were like ghosts of the jungle.

On November 13, 1944, the U.S. Naval Governor's appointed Police Chief Navy Lieutenant Jon Wigg, issued a formal order to hunt them down. The memorandum directed all members of the Guam Police Department to investigate every rumor, sighting, and trail. Patrols were organized out of Agana and outposts. They seized or destroyed all the evidence of enemy life, shelter, food, and clothing. The mission was blunt and dangerous: track and capture, or eliminate the hidden enemy combatants.

Thus began the freedom fighter group known as the Guam Combat Patrol. A team of native Chamoru men from the Guam Police Department who volunteered for one of the most perilous military duties. The continued liberation of Guam. Operating in hostile terrain against an unseen and unpredictable enemy. They were hunters of men. The Guam

Combat Patrol was an active duty designated trained fighting force formally attached to the U.S. Marine Corps.

Led by Police Staff Sergeant Juan U. Aguon, the Patrol comprised 15 original members: Joaquin S. Aguon, Vicente L. Borja, Jose S. Bukikosa, Francisco J. Cruz, George G. Flores, Roman N. Ignacio, Antonio P. Pangelinan, Agapito S. Perez, Pedro A. Perez, Ignacio R. Rivera, Jose P. Salas, Pedro R. San Nicolas, Jose S. Tenorio, and Felix C. Wusstig.

Later, augmented by other brave volunteers, 14 other police officers joined the Patrol. They were: Edward G. Aflague, Joaquin M. Camacho, Felix T. Cruz, Jose D. Cruz, Mariano C. Cruz, Vicente Q. Duenas, Francisco C. Leon Guerrero, David L. Lujan, Juan L. Lujan, Charles H. McDonald, Antonio C. Perez, Juan A. Quinata, Pedro C. Santos, and Alfred F. Taitano. These men operated as both law enforcers and combat troops. They tracked enemy soldiers across every corner of the island.

Their work was relentless and lethal. Throughout their missions, the Guam Combat Patrol was relentless and lethal. They killed over 117 Japanese soldiers, captured 5, and forced many others to flee, starve, or die in hiding. Their daring operations often came at high stakes. The Guam Combat Patrol lost 2 members. Antonio P. Manibusan and Pedro R. San Nicolas. Several others were wounded, including Vicente Borja, Joaquin S. Aguon, Juan L. Lujan, and George Flores.

In Talofofo on May 1, 1945, a supposedly dead Japanese soldier threw a grenade, wounding Borja and Flores. In Dededo, an enemy soldier shot Lujan in the leg. These isolated skirmishes varied and were the daily risks of their mission. The patrol leader, Staff Sergeant Juan U. Aguon, received the Silver Star from President Harry S. Truman for his bravery and leadership.

All members of the Guam Combat Patrol received the Bronze Star. In November 1948, after 4 years of relentless service, the authorities disbanded the Guam Combat Patrol. Their legacy, however, continues to this day. It is etched in the survival of a people, the freedom of our island, and the enduring spirit of Chamoru resilience.

These men were not just police.

They were warriors.

They were protectors.

They were liberators.

They were family members.

They were sons of Guåhan.

Chapter 5: Continued Liberation with GCP

Cruz in uniform at Nimitz Hill Guns. (Photo credit: Personal Collection)

Chapter 5: Continued Liberation with GCP

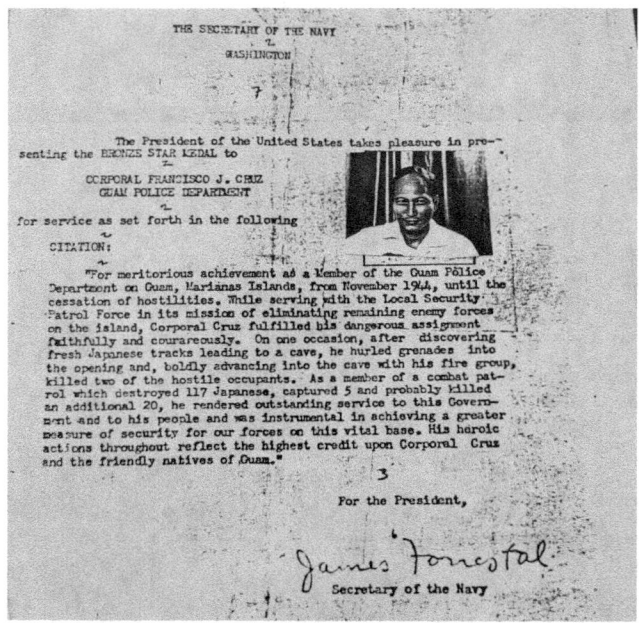

Cruz's Bronze Star award from combat actions with the Guam Combat
Patrol (Photo credit: Personal Collection)

Chapter 5: Continued Liberation with GCP

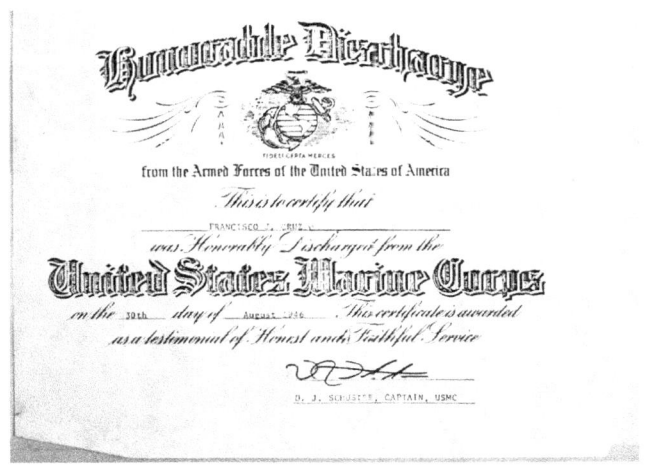

Cruz's U.S.M.C Honorable Discharge. (Photo credit: Personal Collection)
The appearance of U.S. Department of Defense (DoD) visual information does
not imply or constitute DoD endorsement.

Chapter 5: Continued Liberation with GCP

Cruz walking out of a cave after an inspection while Jose Tenorio protects the patrol from attacks above. July 1945. (Photo: National Archives)

Chapter 5: Continued Liberation with GCP

Guam Combat Patrol members in this photo are Joaquin S. Aguon, Vicente L. Borja, Jose S. Bukikosa, Francisco J. Cruz (Far Right), George G. Flores, Roman N. Ignacio, Antonio Manibusan, Agapito S. Perez, Pedro A. Perez, Ignacio R. Rivera, Jose P. Salas, Pedro R. San Nicolas, Fred Taitano, and Felix C. Wusstig. (Photo Courtesy of the National Park Services)

Chapter 5: Continued Liberation with GCP

Guam Combat Patrol parade photo. Cruz (Center right) (Photo credit:
Personal Collection)

Chapter 5: Continued Liberation with GCP

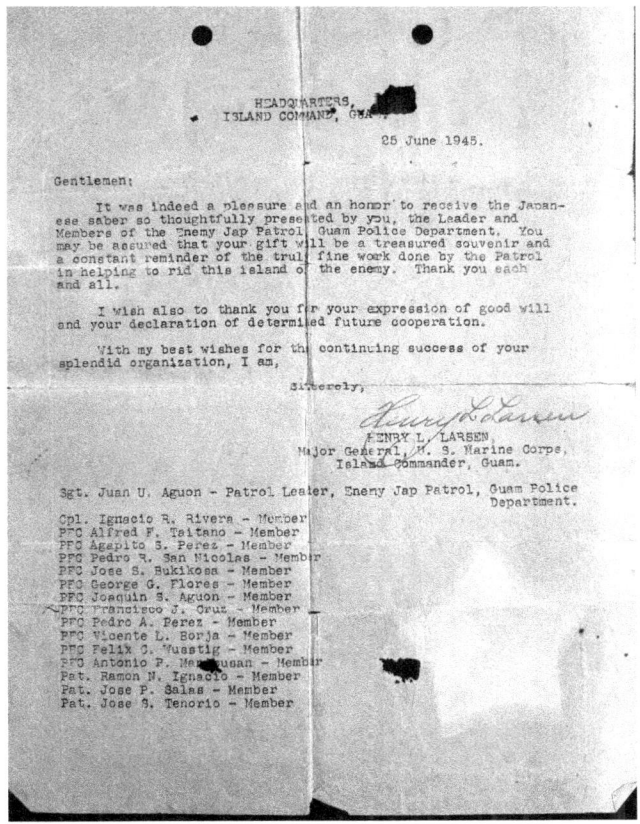

Original Letter from Guam Marine Commander Major General Henry L. Larsen (80 Years old) (Photo credit: Personal Collection)

Chapter 6- Recognition Efforts

Chapter 6: Recognition Efforts

I grew up hearing the stories, fragments of war, and acts of heroism buried under decades of silence. As you read throughout the Liberation of Guam, one of the most important actions needed to help the Americans liberate our island, points back to my great-grandfather, Francisco Jesus Cruz. Who proved that his bravery was indispensable during the Japanese Occupation.

What started as family stories and old photographs soon turned into something far deeper. As I searched through documents, military records, and oral histories, I uncovered efforts throughout the years to receive the once-promised award. Despite receiving the Bronze Star for his combat actions with the GCP. Officials ignored his most vital combat actions which paved the way for the Liberation of Guam. I knew I had to do something.

My journey began not at the round table but in the quiet moments of reflection. This weight began to build knowing a great historical injustice to our people and country would happen if lost. I began writing, speaking, and connecting with historians and elected officials. By compiling testimonies and reconstructing timelines, I brought Cruz's story out of the shadows and into the light. I quickly realized this fight was bigger than one person.

The erasure of Chamoru heroism and the marginalization of Pacific Islanders in the broader narrative of American history needed change. This began my journey in creating the Chamoru American Foundation. It was inspired by not only by my great grandfather Cruz and the Guam

Combat Patrol, but to also give back. As an organization, we stand for every overlooked sacrifice made by the people of the Marianas. We pursue justice, remembrance, and preparedness. This by uplifting our stories, building resilience for the future, and ensuring our heroes' names would never be lost again.

Through the foundation, our core mission to increase emergency preparedness for the Mariana Islands. We strive to build lasting partnerships that help to protect our most isolated communities. Every preparedness item delivered, event, program, and handshake is an act of honoring my great-grandfather and all who stood like him. We give back by preparing the islands for tomorrow's emergencies while remembering past battles.

This fight for the Medal of Honor is not about medals. It's about recognition. It's about representation. It's about ensuring that when America writes the story of its greatest heroes, it includes those who bled for it from its furthest edges.

Chapter 6: Recognition Efforts

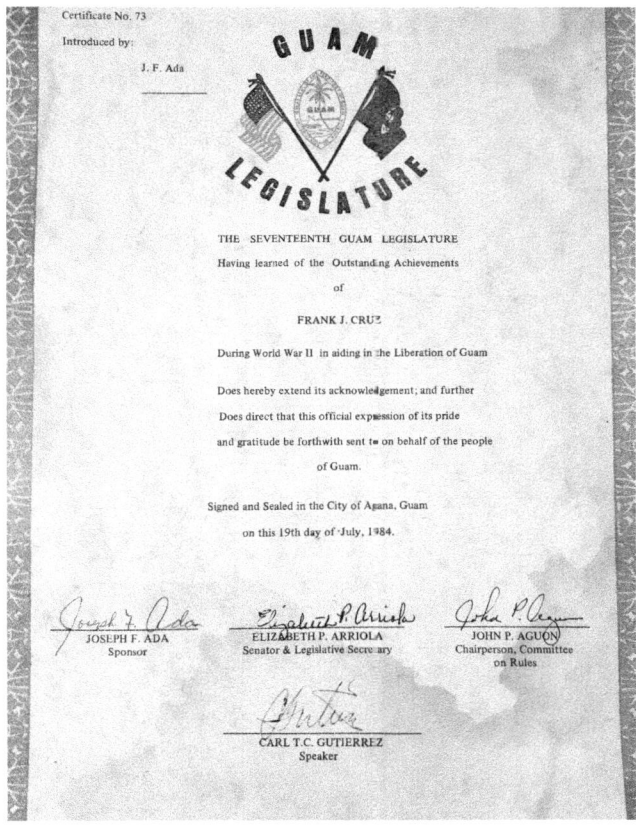

Guam Legislature (17th) honoring Cruz's MOH heroics (Photo credit: Personal Collection)

Chapter 6: Recognition Efforts

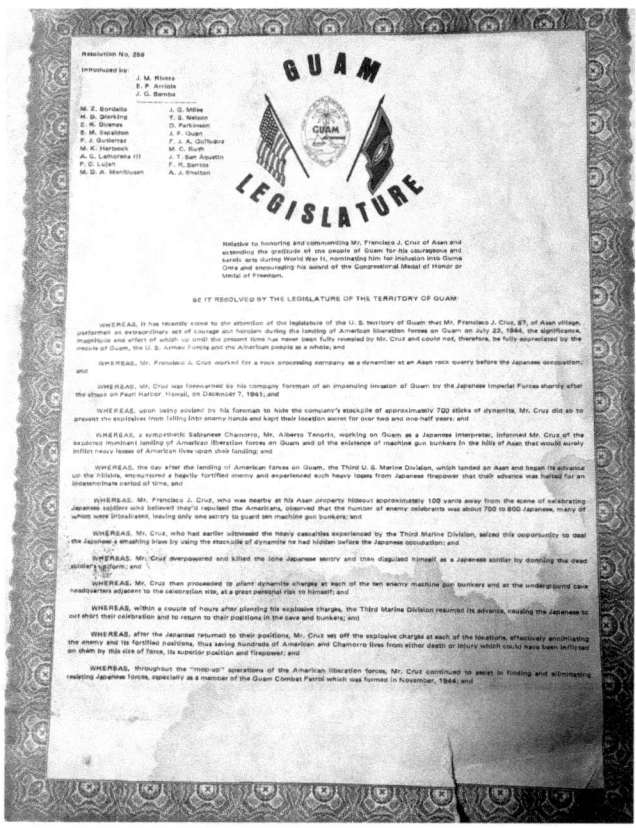

Guam Legislature (19th) honoring Cruz's MOH heroics (Photo credit: Personal Collection)

Chapter 6: Recognition Efforts

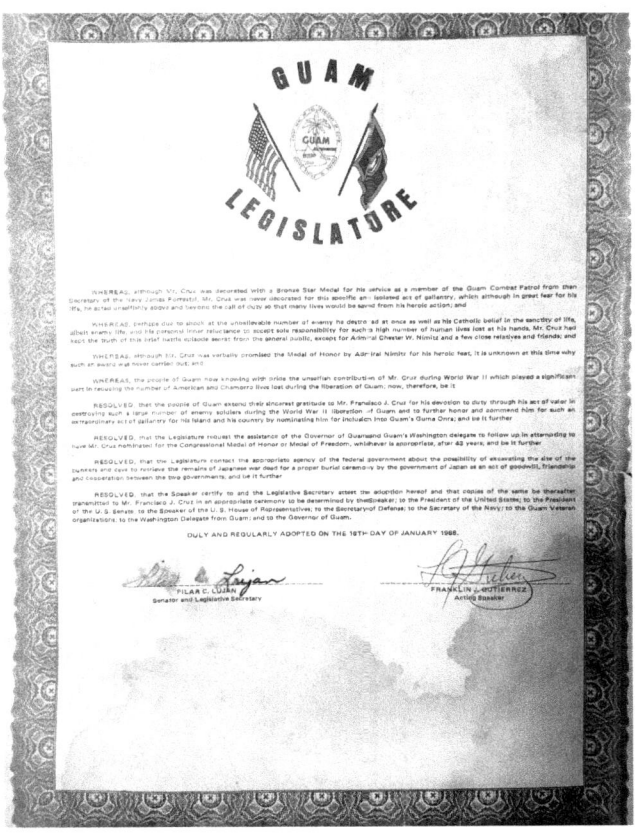

Guam Legislature (19th) honoring Cruz's MOH heroics (Photo credit:
Personal Collection)

Chapter 6: Recognition Efforts

Cruz receiving certificate of appreciation from Governor Ricardo J. Bordallo (Photo credit: Personal Collection)

Chapter 6: Recognition Efforts

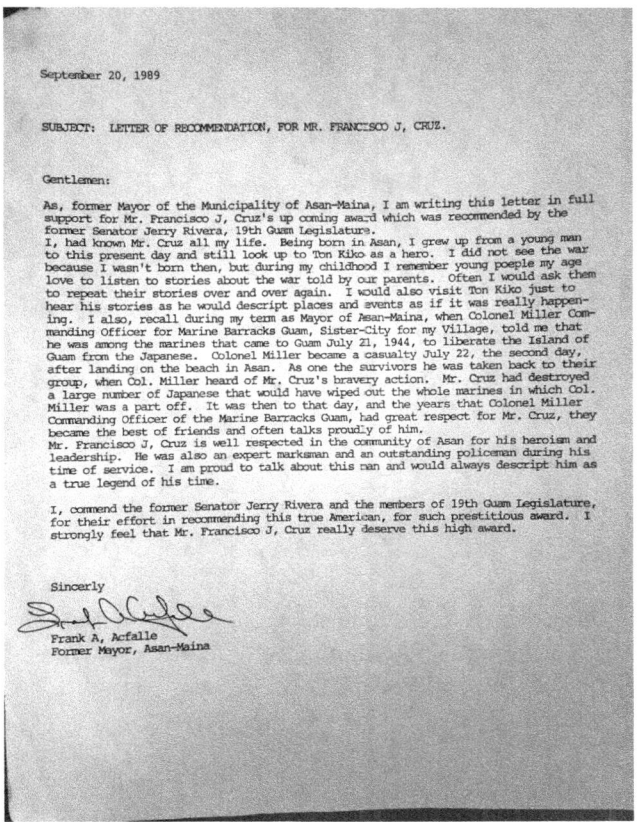

September 20, 1989

SUBJECT: LETTER OF RECOMMENDATION, FOR MR. FRANCISCO J, CRUZ.

Gentlemen:

As, former Mayor of the Municipality of Asan-Maina, I am writing this letter in full
support for Mr. Francisco J, Cruz's up coming award which was recommended by the
former Senator Jerry Rivera, 19th Guam Legislature.
I, had known Mr. Cruz all my life. Being born in Asan, I grew up from a young man
to this present day and still look up to Ton Kiko as a hero. I did not see the war
because I wasn't born then, but during my childhood I remember young poeple my age
love to listen to stories about the war told by our parents. Often I would ask them
to repeat their stories over and over again. I would also visit Ton Kiko just to
hear his stories as he would descript places and events as if it was really happen-
ing. I also, recall during my term as Mayor of Asan-Maina, when Colonel Miller Commanding Officer for Marine Barracks Guam, Sister-City for my Village, told me that
he was among the marines that came to Guam July 21, 1944, to liberate the Island of
Guam from the Japanese. Colonel Miller became a casualty July 22, the second day,
after landing on the beach in Asan. As one the survivors he was taken back to their
group, when Col. Miller heard of Mr. Cruz's bravery action. Mr. Cruz had destroyed
a large number of Japanese that would have wiped out the whole marines in which Col.
Miller was a part off. It was then to that day, and the years that Colonel Miller
Commanding Officer of the Marine Barracks Guam, had great respect for Mr. Cruz, they
became the best of friends and often talks proudly of him.
Mr. Francisco J, Cruz is well respected in the community of Asan for his heroism and
leadership. He was also an expert marksman and an outstanding policeman during his
time of service. I am proud to talk about this man and would always descript him as
a true legend of his time.

I, commend the former Senator Jerry Rivera and the members of 19th Guam Legislature,
for their effort in recommending this true American, for such prestitious award. I
strongly feel that Mr. Francisco J, Cruz really deserve this high award.

Sincerly

Frank A, Acfalle
Former Mayor, Asan-Maina

Medal of Honor Letter of Recommendation from Former Mayor of Asan.
(Photo credit: Personal Collection)

Chapter 6: Recognition Efforts

The Guam Combat Patrol statue at the Governors complex at Adelup on Guam. Cruz is the one pointing surrounded by U.S. Marines. (Photo credit: Personal Collection)

Chapter 6: Recognition Efforts

Cruz with his statue (Photo credit: Personal Collection)

Chapter 6: Recognition Efforts

Former members of the Guam Combat Patrol await presentation of the Asiatic-Pacific Campaign Medal and the World War II Victory Medal. (National Archives Identifier 6392711) Cruz is second from left.

Chapter 6: Recognition Efforts

Cruz getting pinned his medals. (Photo credit: Personal Collection)

Chapter 7- Chamoru Legacy

Chapter 7: Chamoru Legacy

The story of my great-grandfathers bravery is more than a family memory. It is a mirror reflecting the unshakable strength of the Chamoru people and the enduring spirit of all Pacific Islanders who stood their ground during World War II. His acts of resistance, loyalty, and sacrifice during the Japanese Occupation of Guam embody not just personal heroism but the broader collective courage of the entire Chamoru population that refused to be broken.

To the Chamoru people, my great-grandfathers story is monumental. It affirms our place in a war too often told without us. It is another example that proves we were not merely passive victims of occupation but active participants in the fight for our homeland. Though unfulfilled, Admiral Chester Nimitz's promise of the Medal of Honor to my great-grandfather still stands as a symbol of the valor that Chamorus brought to one of the world's darkest hours.

For Pacific Islanders across Oceania, this story resonates deeply. The islands of the Pacific were not just battlegrounds, they were homes. Indigenous people in the Marianas, Micronesia, Polynesia, and Melanesia bore the brutal weight of war, often without protection. Frequently overlooked by their colonizers and liberators alike. Yet, we endured. We resisted, aided wounded soldiers, shared food with strangers, and protected families with everything available. Their courage may not fill textbooks, but it lives in every scar on these islands and every family member after them.

Chapter 7: Chamoru Legacy

To America, Cruz's combat actions and promise of the Medal of Honor are a challenge and a reminder. Expanding the lens of history and recognizing the sacrifices made by those outside the continental United States is a challenge. This reminds us that loyalty transcends citizenship and that bravery exists even in the most remote parts of the American family. Since the early 1930s, Chamorus fought for this nation (Not citizens yet), and we continue to fight for our country. Guam is not a footnote. The Chamoru people are not an asterisk. We are American, we are Chamoru American.

The legacy left behind by Cruz and his fellow island patriots was not just historical, but generational. It lives in our language, the strength of our elders, the resilience of our youth, and the spirit of every Chamoru who wakes up knowing that we come from fighters. It inspires young islanders to walk taller, to speak louder, and to demand recognition with dignity. We teach our children our stories, not to dwell in pain, but to remind them we came from ancient, proud, and powerful people.

Chapter 7: Chamoru Legacy

We stand on the shoulders of giants who walked barefoot through war zones, who hid soldiers in their homes, who faced execution with their heads held high. Their strength flows through us like ocean currents. We are the legacy of the generations that refused to vanish.

One day, we hope to place the Medal of Honor where it rightfully belongs. Not only to honor my great grandfather but to also honor all Chamorus who fought without medals, recognition, and in fear. Until that day comes, we will keep telling this story. Not for revenge, not for vanity, but for truth. As for now, he will forever be the deadliest Chamoru American warrior in our nation and peoples history.

Chapter 7: Chamoru Legacy

This is a photo of Cruz and his wife donating the Japanese rifle he captured while on patrol during the liberation of Guam, to the Guam National Guard. This rifle is on display at the Guam Museum as the Japanese rifle donated from the GNG. The person accepting the gift is the former Adjutant General, Brig. Gen. Frank C. Torres. (Photo Credit: Guam National Guard) The appearance of U.S. Department of Defense (DoD) visual information does not imply or constitute DoD endorsement.

Chapter 7: Chamoru Legacy

Cruz receiving his Certificate of Appreciation from the Guam National Guard. (Photo credit: Personal Collection) The appearance of the U.S. Department of Defense (DoD) visual information does not imply or constitute DoD endorsement.

Chapter 6: Chamoru Legacy

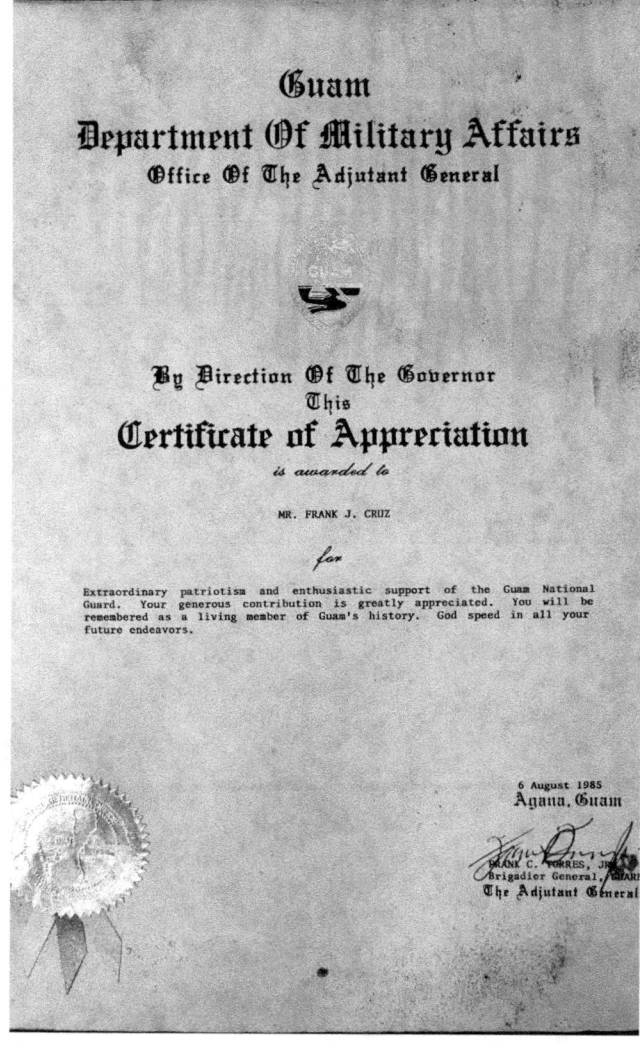

Certificate of Appreciation from the Guam National Guard. (Photo credit: Personal Collection)

Chamoru American Foundation

C.A.F:

The Chamoru American Foundation is a 501(C)(3) nonprofit organization whose mission is to serve, protect, and increase the emergency preparedness of the Mariana Islands, the most geographically isolated inhabited territory of the United States. From Guam to the rest of the Northern Marianas, we aim to keep these strategically vital but often overlooked islands from being left behind during crises. With every purchase of this book, a portion of the proceeds contributes to that mission.

Inspired by the heroism of the Guam Combat Patrol and my great-grandfather. This foundation was born from a legacy of sacrifice, resilience, and resistance. Cruz and the Guam Combat Patrol (GCP) were vital to the U.S. Marines during the Liberation of Guam in World War II and saved countless lives.

Through that legacy, we honor all warfighters who defended our homeland. Today, we continue that spirit of service by building partnerships and resilience, training communities, securing critical resources, and creating rapid-response capabilities for the islands' most pressing emergency needs, terrorist attacks, natural disasters, supply chain disruptions, and climate threats. The Chamoru American Foundation stands as a modern shield for the Mariana Islands, rooted in the past but ready for the future.

Follow us on Instagram for Medal of Honor updates or preparedness tips:

@ChamoruAmericanFndn

To support directly, donate to the URL below:

HTTPS://WWW.CHAMORUAMERICAN.ORG

Dedication

Dedication:

To my great-grandfather, whose heroic sacrifices and promised Medal of Honor have inspired this journey of truth, remembrance, and justice.

To the brave men of the Guam Combat Patrol, our native warriors who risked everything to take on the fight and fully liberate our homeland.

To the United States military, whose strength and sacrifice helped liberate our islands and people and restore the light of freedom.

To all the native Chamorus who suffered, resisted, or perished during the dark years of occupation, your courage echoes through generations and will endure.

This book aims to serve as a tribute to peace born from great sacrifice and for all lost in the war's fires across every land and side.

Coming Soon

Coming Soon:

While the release of this book honoring the GCP and my great-grandfather's Medal of Honor heroics marks a milestone in telling his wartime story, it is only the beginning. As I work to bring Cruz's heroic actions to light, I realized there was a much deeper narrative waiting to be told. That is why I have begun working on a second, more comprehensive project.

The complete biography of Francisco Jesus Cruz. The man behind the legacy. This upcoming book will not just document his battlefield valor but also illuminate his life before and after the war. His roots as a proud Chamoru son of Guam. His leadership during the Japanese Occupation. His role in the Guam Combat Patrol. The impact he had on his family, village, people, and island.

I want the world to know not just the warrior who earned the Medal of Honor's promise and helped Liberate Guam. I also want to share his life as a father, grandfather, great-grandfather, protector, and symbol of resistance. This biography will feature newly uncovered historical records and oral histories never shared publicly. It is a deeply personal journey that feels like a responsibility to share as a tribute.

The upcoming biography will serve as a companion to this book. Expanding the portrait of a man who exemplified the strength, pride, and resilience of the Chamoru people. I hope this next chapter in Francisco Cruz's story not only honors his life but inspires future generations. Inspires them to carry forward his spirit of service, sacrifice, and love for his islands and people.

Credits

Credits:

National Archives. "Online Website" At link: https://www.archives.gov/

The War in the Pacific-National Park Service. "Combat Patrol hunts for stragglers" Accessed Online. At link: https://www.nps.gov/parkhistory/online_books/npswapa/extcontent/lib/liberation27.htm

First Edition

ISBN:

ISBN-13: 979-8-9993736-1-8

www.ingramcontent.com/pod-product-compliance
Lightning Source LLC
Chambersburg PA
CBHW060058150626
46556CB00017BA/2016